Daily Mirror

Part of the Mirror Collection
Head of Syndication & Licensing: **Fergus McKenna**
Mirrorpix: **David Scripps, Simon Flavin, John Mead,
Paul Mason, Vito Inglese**
020 7293 3858

Produced by Trinity Mirror Media
PO BOX 48, Liverpool L69 3EB

Managing Director: **Ken Rogers**
Publishing Director: **Steve Hanrahan**
Executive Art Editor: **Rick Cooke**
Senior Editor: **Paul Dove**
Compiled and written by: **Alan Jewell**
Designed and produced by: **Roy Gilfoyle**

© Published by Trinity Mirror 2014
Images: Mirrorpix
Printed by PCP

HOW BEATLEMANIA ELECTRIFIED A NATION

Tours turned The Beatles into biggest band in the world

Half a century has passed since The Beatles made their historic first visit to the United States and, in doing so, changed the face of popular music.

No other act has made such an impact on the States, before or since. It was extraordinary, unprecedented and remains unmatched.

The arrival of John, Paul, George and Ringo in New York in February 1964 helped lift the mood of a nation still coming to terms with the assassination of their president, John F Kennedy, less than two months earlier.

Shock, grief, anger and fear were the dominant emotions in the US until the four lads from Liverpool turned up to spark excitement and hysteria in American teenagers.

The Beatles' popularity grew bigger and bigger in Britain throughout 1963, to the extent that the term 'Beatlemania' was coined to describe the phenomenon infecting the UK.

America remained immune and ignorant at what was happening across the pond for most of the year, largely because Capitol Records, owned by EMI, did not release their singles in the States, believing The Beatles would hold little or no appeal to a country which they believed had moved beyond rock and roll.

When The Beatles began to garner some attention in the US, bemused news reports focused on the giddy effect their music was having on the British people, rather than the songs or the lads producing them.

They were first seen on American television screens on November 18 1963, as NBC's *The Huntley-Brinkley Report* ran a four-minute item on Beatlemania. Four days later CBS's *Evening News* was scheduled to follow suit but the broadcast was cancelled following the killing of Kennedy that lunchtime. The film was eventually shown on December 10, and ▶

BEHIND THE SCENES: Ringo takes a photo of Paul on the set of The Ed Sullivan Show

▶ played a significant part in increasing interest in the group, which, in turn, belatedly sparked Capitol into action. The single *I Want To Hold Your Hand* was rush-released on December 26, providing the commercial breakthrough.

The Beatles themselves were wary of visiting the US, fearing that the American people would simply not be interested. Paul McCartney, in particular, was fearful of embarrassment, telling manager Brian Epstein that they shouldn't go over until they had a number one in the States.

They timed the visit perfectly, as they learned *I Want To Hold Your Hand* had reached top spot just days before they flew over. But McCartney was still uneasy, telling legendary producer Phil Spector on the plane: "They've got their own groups. What are we going to give them that they don't already have?"

He needn't have worried. Sent on their way with the best wishes of thousands of devoted fans at Heathrow, they were greeted by a similarly-sized crowd at the newly-named John F Kennedy Airport in New York when Pan Am Flight 101 reached its destination.

The airport, and indeed America, had never seen anything like it. Hundreds of journalists were also waiting for them, and as they wisecracked their way through a chaotic press conference, the fresh-faced mop-tops began to appreciate that they were already hugely popular.

A massive promotional campaign in advance had stoked interest and with *I Want To Hold Your Hand* receiving heavy radio airplay, America was desperate to get to know John Lennon, Paul McCartney, George Harrison and Ringo Starr.

From the airport they got into individual limousines and were driven to the Plaza Hotel in Manhattan, where another large crowd of fans awaited them.

Two days later they made their first live television appearance in the US, on *The Ed Sullivan Show*. It proved to be an historic occasion in American popular culture, influencing generations of musicians who followed in their wake.

As Tom Petty memorably put it: "The Beatles came on *The Ed Sullivan Show* and it was like the whole world changed overnight."

> '*The Beatles came on The Ed Sullivan Show and it was like the whole world changed overnight*'

WARM WELCOME: A cavalcade of cars and motorbikes transports The Beatles on their arrival in Los Angeles in August 1964

IN DEMAND: The Beatles face the media shortly after landing in America for their first tour in the country

Manager Epstein had struck a shrewd deal for The Beatles to be given top billing on Sullivan's show for three consecutive weeks. Sullivan had initially offered a large payment for a single appearance, but Epstein negotiated increased exposure for a reduced fee. The group opened and closed all three shows. While it would be impossible to put a value on this arrangement, Epstein's foresight was inspired.

Sullivan opened the broadcast by announcing: "Tonight, the whole country is waiting to hear England's Beatles." If that statement was an exaggeration, it was only a slight one.

That first electrifying performance, recorded at CBS Studio 50 in front of shrieking, screaming teenagers, was watched by 73 million people, at the time the largest television audience ever recorded in the US. According to the *New York Daily News*, 'never in American history had so many young people screamed so hard at exactly the same moment'. A nation was in thrall to The Beatles' dazzling talent and cheeky charm.

The significance of the Sullivan performance was marked by the recent reuniting of the surviving members of the group, McCartney and Starr, at a special concert entitled: *The Night That Changed America: A Grammy Salute To The Beatles*.

Recorded at the same studio (now renamed the Ed Sullivan Theater) on January 27 2014, it was scheduled for broadcast by CBS for ▶

Daily Mirror

Goodbye, Britain—then the Big Hello

Fans on a roof at London Airport wave goodbye to the Beatles yesterday.

3d. Saturday, February 8, 1964 No. 18,704

YEAH! YEAH! U.S.A!

That old Beatlemania hits New York as a screaming girl tries to reach the Beatles.

Paul, Ringo, George and John answer questions at the Press conference.

IRENE GOES HOME TODAY

PRINCESS Irene of Holland, whose romance has started a constitutional crisis, is going home today.

This was announced in the Hague last night by the Dutch Government.

Retreat

The announcement added that Irene—who recently became a Roman Catholic—had been spending several days in a house of retreat" in Spain.

A second Government statement denied rumours that Queen Juliana might

'Some good news soon'

abdicate because of differences with the Cabinet over the romance.

Meanwhile Holland's Crown Princess Beatrix and her sister Margriet returned home yesterday from Austria, where they have been watching the winter Olympics.

Their father, Prince Bernhard, flew his own

plane to Austria to collect them.

Meanwhile, in Madrid, Irene's secretary said that she " will soon be able to announce some good news in respect of her private life."

Overcome

It went on: " The princess has overcome the difficulties she had encountered in her spirit."

The statement denied that 24-year-old Irene's suitor was Prince Alfonso de Bourbon, grandson of the last King of Spain.

From BARRIE HARDING
New York, Friday

FIVE thousand screaming, chanting teenagers—most of them playing truant from school —gave the Beatles a fantastic welcome here today.

More than 100 extra police were on duty to control the crowd as the group's jet landed at the John F. Kennedy Airport.

'Mad'

Pandemonium broke out among the stamping, banner-waving fans as the Beatles—John Lennon, Paul McCartney, George Harrison and Ringo Starr—stepped from the plane.

One policeman who has worked at the airport for ten years said : " I think the world has gone mad."

5,000 scream 'welcome' to the Beatles

And a veteran airport employee said : " I see it—but I don't believe it."

Then, when the group had left the plane, thousands of their screaming fans rushed to the balcony above the Customs Hall to watch them pass through.

There were screams and shouts as their guitars appeared on a luggage trolley.

There were fresh squeals as the Beatles finally appeared, surrounded by a " bodyguard " of New York policemen.

Fans waved huge posters. There was a huge banner

which proclaimed " Welcome to Beatlesville, U.S.A."

One of the fans had travelled 1,500 miles from Arkansas to see the group arrive—and many more had travelled up to 300 miles.

Airport officials said the crowd rivalled anything since General MacArthur returned from Korea.

The airport Press conference which followed the Beatles' arrival was chaos.

Hundreds of reporters and photographers, plus seven TV cameras, had the room bursting at its seams.

Part of the question-and-

answer session between reporters and Beatles went like this:

" Will you sing something ? "

John Lennon : " No ! "

" Can you sing ? "

" Not without money "

" How much money do you expect to make in the USA ? "

George Harrison : " About half a crown."

" Are you going to get haircuts ? "

Lennon : " we had one yesterday."

Hits

They were also asked what they thought of an anti-Beatle campaign in the mid-West, where some motorists were exhibiting stickers saying : " Stamp Out The Beatles."

Lennon replied : " We have a campaign to stamp out Detroit."

● The Beatles were told just before leaving London that their records " I Wanna Hold Your Hand " and " She Loves You " were joint No. 1 in the US Hit Parade

BIG NEWS: The Daily Mirror front page from February 1964 illustrates how Beatlemania gripped America

February 9, the 50th anniversary of that historic first TV performance.

Paul and Ringo performed several Beatles classics, while a host of musicians took to the stage to play songs by the Fab Four, including Stevie Wonder, Alicia Keys, Dave Grohl, Pharrell Williams, Annie Lennox, Katy Perry, Jeff Lynne and George Harrison's son, Dhani.

Grohl, of the Foo Fighters, paid his own tribute by observing: "The Beatles are the foundation of everything we do."

Speaking during the show, Paul admitted: "When I was asked to do this show, I was wondering if it was the right thing to do. Was it seemly to tribute yourself? Then I saw a couple of American guys and they said, 'You don't understand the enormous impact that show (the *Ed Sullivan* performance) had on America.' So then I understood and I decided to show up."

Of course, that initial outing on *The Ed Sullivan Show* in February 1964 was merely the start of The Beatles' performances in America.

During that first two-week visit they performed just two concerts, in Washington and New York, outside their *Ed Sullivan* commitments, but their every movement and utterance was given huge import by the British and American media who trailed after them, while devoted fans attempted all manner of scams to get close to them.

SCREAM AND SHOUT: A fan on the streets of New York is overcome with excitement

By the time the first visit was over, there was no doubt that The Beatles had conquered America, as they led the British invasion of bands that enjoyed significant success in the States. They were given a heroes' welcome on their return to Britain.

They were back in North America in August 1964 for a full, month-long tour, performing 30 concerts in 24 cities across the US and Canada. Their fame and success had grown even bigger in the meantime (in April 1964 they held the first five spots on the Billboard Singles chart) as The Beatles accomplished, in the words of *Rolling Stone* magazine, 'the largest victory in rock & roll history'.

This special anniversary celebration relives the excitement of those first two triumphant visits, featuring rare and unseen images, plus day-by-day reports and diaries which were published in the *Daily Mirror* and *Liverpool Echo* and include the thoughts of John, Paul, George and Ringo as the madness unfolded around them.

The February 1964 trip to America marked the moment The Beatles unquestionably became the biggest band in the world. Fifty years later, and 44 years after they broke up, it's a status that they still hold.

OUT OF CONTROL: One hysterical fan is carried away by police in Vancouver

HERE THEY COME: A sign in the window of Grimbles Store on 33rd Street in New York heralds The Beatles' arrival

THE OTHER GEORGE HARRISON

THE LOST TOUR DIARY

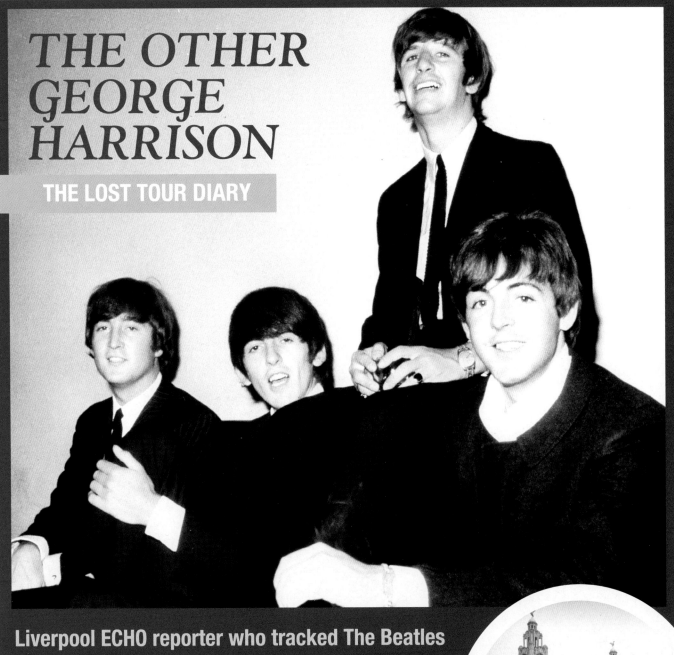

Liverpool ECHO reporter who tracked The Beatles on their all-conquering North American tours

It was quite a quirk that the reporter the *Liverpool Echo* sent to the US to cover The Beatles' visits to America shared a name with one of the band members.

The *Echo*'s George Harrison (pictured, right) was among the evening newspaper's most prominent journalists and was at the forefront of chronicling the emerging Merseybeat scene in the early 1960s.

Through this role, he came to know the Beatles well, earning their trust to the extent that they spoke to him regularly during the American adventures, providing great insight for readers in the city where they originated.

In the course of researching this publication, we discovered Harrison's original diary reports in the *Liverpool Echo* office, a diary that had not been published for nearly 50 years.

George Harrison the journalist was best known for his *Over the Mersey Wall* column, which appeared daily on page two of the *Echo*, showing Harrison wearing his trademark trilby leaning over a graphic of a wall. It was a column full of gossip and short human stories, often revealing who was getting a record contract or who was switching groups.

The Beatle George Harrison paid tribute to his namesake by calling an experimental instrumental on his second solo album *Under the Mersey Wall*.

Many of Harrison's daily diaries from the February and August/September 1964 visits are reproduced in this celebratory magazine, providing a flavour of how a Liverpool native viewed the hysteria that surrounded The Beatles as they trekked from coast to coast.

They go behind the scenes into what was happening within the Beatles' party as they attempted to navigate their way through the pandemonium that followed their progress.

The wit and flippancy of the Fab Four shines through, although it is also abundantly clear how seriously they took their music.

Harrison notes the struggles of American police and security officers as they attempt to maintain some semblance of control while thousands of delirious fans swarm around The Beatles.

The reports are a fascinating record of history in the making.

THE BEATLES IN THE USA, WINTER 1964

February 9: *The Ed Sullivan Show, CBS Studio 50, New York City*
February 11: *Washington Coliseum*
February 12: *Carnegie Hall, New York City*
February 16: *The Ed Sullivan Show, Deauville Hotel, Miami*
February 23 (recorded on February 9): *The Ed Sullivan Show, CBS Studio 50, New York City*

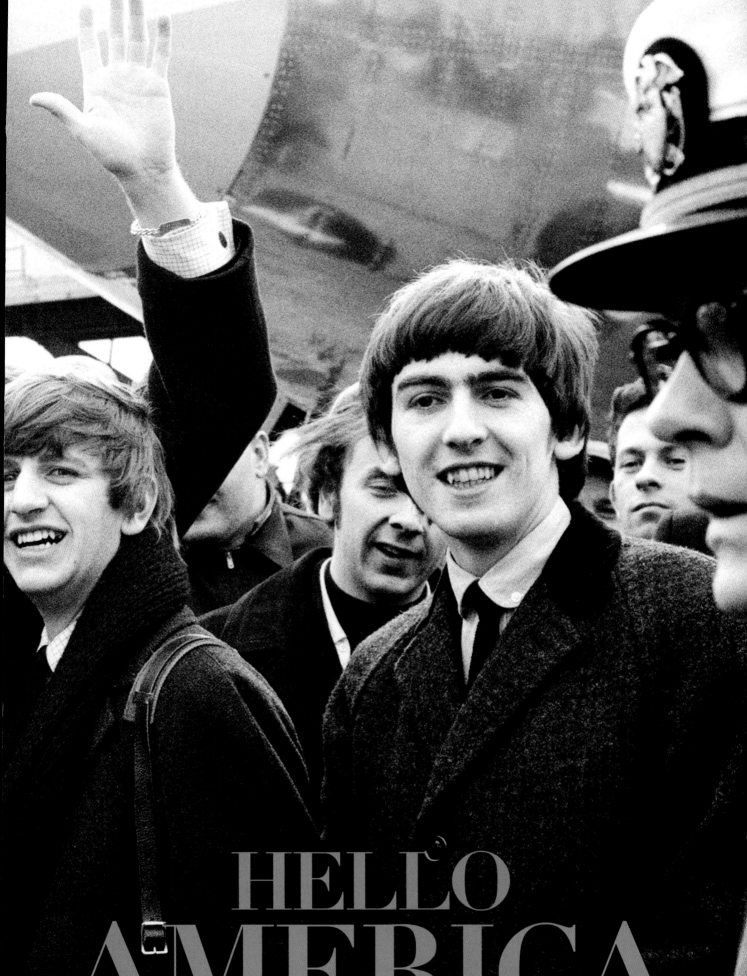

HELLO AMERICA

The Beatles hit number one in time for New York arrival

FRIDAY, FEBRUARY 7 – There were fantastic scenes at London Airport today as Liverpool's Beatles left in a Boeing jet, all set to conquer America.

As they walked to the aircraft, hundreds of love-letters, badges, photographs, jelly babies and loads of fan mail rained down from the spectators' gallery on the roof of the transatlantic departure terminal building.

Screams drowned the noise of the huge jets taking off nearby.

Before they boarded their aircraft, the boys posed for photographers, nervously twiddled fingers, smoked cigarettes and signed autographs for airport and airline staff.

Paul said: "Yes, we are a bit nervous. We are not worried about the crowds – we just hope that we go down well over there."

But they need have had no fears, for a few minutes before they left a message was flashed from New York to manager Brian Epstein at London Airport.

It read: 'Congratulations. The records *She Loves You* and *I Want To Hold Your Hand* have today reached joint No. 1 position.'

Travelling with the group and their manager is John Lennon's wife, Cynthia. She hung in the background, shyly talking to friends. "I'm nervous and excited at the same time," was her only comment.

The Beatles were due to arrive in New York at 18.40 GMT to begin their hectic 10-day invasion of the United States.

Police have made special arrangements to deal with demonstrations by teenagers, who have been whipped into a frenzy of anticipation by repeated playing of their records by America's disc jockeys.

HERE WE GO: Four Liverpool lads and their team board the plane to New York

FLIGHT OF FANTASY: John, wife Cynthia and producer Phil Spector relax on the plane, George gets his camera ready and a stewardess helps the boys relax on the flight to New York

THE LOST TOUR DIARY

An amazing welcome to 'Beatletown'

This staggered city is still wondering exactly what hit it yesterday when four shaggy-haired lads from Liverpool, The Beatles, arrived to whip up a teenage tornado such as it had never before experienced.

Over a four-column front-page picture of John, Paul, George and Ringo waving a greeting to squealing, yelling youngsters at Kennedy International Airport, the newspaper *Journal American* sums up the whole breathtaking affair by declaring simply, in big type: 'It's Beatletown USA'.

No doubt about it, The Beatles have captured New York and replaced its cynical

dubious 'Oh yeah?' with an emphatic 'Yeah, yeah, yeah!' that's ripping through this morning's brisk Manhattan air.

For already, the kids are grouping again for a second day's affectionate offensive outside our Plaza Hotel in plush Fifth Avenue.

But the Beatles are still sleeping after last night's late sightseeing on Broadway. Today they face rehearsals for tomorrow night's appearance on the Ed Sullivan television show, which is the top guest programme in the United States, watched by millions.

The scenes when the Beatles arrived at the newly-named John Kennedy International Airport (which used to be Idlewind) were the first big shock for New Yorkers.

Expert estimates put the

Continued page 17

A WARM WELCOME: Fans line the streets of New York to welcome their English visitors while (right) Paul, Ringo, George and John keep the assembled media at John F Kennedy Airport amused

SETTLING IN:
The lads take a seat at the Plaza Hotel after (below) collecting their luggage at the airport

'In 10 years of duty on arrivals of important visitors I have never seen anything like this'

'A greater reception than the President'

From page 15

crowd of teenage girls and boys, who waited hours to welcome them, at roughly 3,000.

It sounded like twice that number as they screamed, whistled, cheered and shouted, "We love you, yeah, yeah, yeah!" from the visitors' gallery and from the balcony inside the airport building.

More than 100 police had been specially brought in to control crowds, but had a tough job. One perspiring sergeant told me: "In 10 years of duty on arrivals of important visitors, I have never seen anything like this. Nobody – not even the President of the United States – ever had a reception to beat these Beatles."

Girls tried to tear press cards from reporters to use themselves, but were fought off.

Among the seething mob of youngsters were some older men carrying posters announcing 'Beatles are starving barbers'.

John Lennon pointed the posters out to the others as, with a 10-strong police and official escort, they walked between barricades to the main building. The boys all laughed and waved to the standard-bearers.

Police cars escorted the Beatles from the airport to New York, and into another tremendous demonstration.

Outside our hotel, mounted police and wooden barriers on the opposite side of Fifth Avenue controlled hundreds of youngsters, mostly school age, who carried placards: 'We love you. Stay for ever.'

LARK
in the
PARK

PHOTO CALL: Ringo, Paul and John pose for photographers in Central Park

LIFE THROUGH A LENS: Ringo prepares to take a few photos of his own – and creates some shelter to light a cigarette

THE FAB THREE: Paul, John and Ringo line up for photos in Central Park

From Sefton Park to Central Park

Since those fantastic scenes at the airport and outside our Plaza Hotel last Friday, police have been showing great determination to break up any further massing of crowds of fans.

Angry photographers protested vigorously when officers even stopped them taking pictures, as arranged, of the Beatles on famous Fifth Avenue and Broadway against a background of mighty Manhattan skyscrapers.

Despite the fierce arguments of fuming photographers, police remained adamant so the whole party returned to the hotel.

Eventually the picture location was fixed for Central Park, which was almost deserted under a thin mantle of snow, and there, free from police interference, the Beatles posed for the cameras.

But as Ringo drily put it: "We could have got pictures like this in Sefton Park instead of coming all this way."

Admittedly, though, the police have had a tough and often exasperating job, keeping hun-

HORSE PLAY: *Paul, John and Ringo take a carriage ride through Central Park while George took time out to recover from tonsillitis*

dreds of girl fans in check when the Beatles have appeared outdoors.

Their departure from our hotel is invariably the signal for a wild stampede of girls attempting to defy the barricades and mounted police.

The kids try every trick in the book to get into the hotel and try to reach the Beatles in their £1,000-a-week suite on the 12th floor – so far without success.

Inside the hotel a dozen security guards are on watch day and night. The corridor leading to the suite is blocked by two iron-jawed guards who refuse to allow anybody past until okayed by someone in authority.

One thing is certain about all this – the New York Police Department will not be forgetting the Beatles for a long, long time.

THE NIGHT THAT CHANGED THE WORLD

Appearance on The Ed Sullivan Show seen by 70 million

MONDAY, FEBRUARY 10 – An army of squealing girls tottered into a TV studio here on legs wobbly from ecstasy, to see the Beatles on *The Ed Sullivan Show*.

Most of the teenagers had queued for hours in the cold outside the theatre. But inside, the Beatles soon warmed them to fever pitch. There were screams even before the four Liverpool lads appeared.

Ed Sullivan, 61-year-old sportswriter-turned-TV-compere, showed up in a Beatle wig and tried to quieten the girls.

At one stage he stamped his foot with mock severity and threatened: "If you don't shut up, I'll call a barber."

When the curtain went up on their idols, the girls let out a fresh burst of screams. You couldn't hear the Beatles for a long, long time.

FAMOUS MR ED:
Ed Sullivan joins The Beatles
for a few photos in the studio

Liverpool lads strike gold – twice

TUESDAY, FEBRUARY 11 – The Beatles' American bandwagon roared on its record-breaking way yesterday.

The Liverpool boys woke up in their luxury suite this morning after their Ed Sullivan TV show, which was watched by between 65 million and 70 million people, to new honours.

First they were presented with two golden discs – one for their LP *Meet the Beatles*, the other for their single *I Want To Hold Your Hand*.

And Capitol Records announced that both discs had hit the million sales mark quicker than any other in history.

Then John, Paul, George and Ringo signed a contract to make three films for United Artists.

The Beatles stopped the traffic everywhere they went in New York.

Their convoy – consisting of two black Cadillacs sandwiched between police patrol cars and occasionally with escorts of mounted police – sailed swiftly through red traffic lights.

Ed Sullivan's office reported today that three out of four New Yorkers watched last night's show.

The Nielsen rating was 58.8, compared with the show's usual rating of about 25.

WARMING UP:
The band warm up for a massive TV appearance with and without George Harrison. Road manager Neil Aspinall (above) stood in for illness-victim George on one occasion

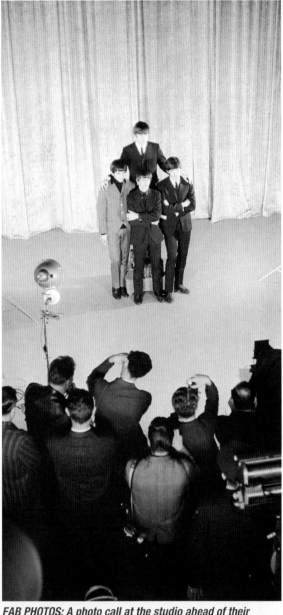

FAB PHOTOS: A photo call at the studio ahead of their *Ed Sullivan Show* appearance

MEN AT WORK: A studio full of people watch rehearsals

THE LOST TOUR DIARY

Super show hits the audience like a bomb

From all over the United States, messages congratulating them on last night's triumphant debut on American television are pouring in on the fabulous Beatles.

In knowledgeable quarters on Broadway, it is being said that their audience on the nationwide *Ed Sullivan Show* will undoubtedly be the biggest in Sullivan's 15 years on television.

Despite George Harrison's attack of tonsillitis, which cut down his singing, the boys hit the packed audience in the studio theatre like a bomb.

The youngsters who comprised most of the lucky 750 who had obtained tickets out of 50,000 applicants screamed,

stamped and even wept in ecstasy at seeing their idols in the flesh. Even older people joined in the storming applause which greeted every song.

Before the show the Beatles were thrilled to receive a cable from Elvis Presley, wishing them luck.

Ed Sullivan said afterwards: "These lads are incredible. I can't remember anything like the reaction they've produced."

Yet, when I met them later, they were not too happy. They complained that John Lennon's microphone hadn't been powerful enough to bring his voice through strongly.

The first three numbers they sang were *All My Loving* followed by Till There Was You and 'She Loves You'.

In the second half of the programme they gave us *I Saw Her Standing There* and *I Want To Hold Your Hand*.

The capital goes crazy for new movie stars

A century and a half or so ago, the British Army burned down Washington, capital city of the United States. Tonight it looks a certainty that four Liverpool lads – those frolicsome Beatles – will burn it up.

As we leave New York, headed for this evening's 8,000 capacity sold-out show in Washington Coliseum, the boys are already aware that the capital is Beatle crazy.

And Lady Ormsby-Gore, wife of the British Ambassador, has sent an invitation to The Beatles to attend her charity ball after the show.

Yesterday the boys received two gold discs to mark million-

dollar sales in America of their long-player *Meet the Beatles* and single record *I Want To Hold Your Hand*. They also signed a contract to appear in three films for United Artists.

John Lennon said to me: "Can we act? We're going to have a bash, but we don't reckon to be a bunch of Richard Burtons."

The national figures of viewers for the Beatles' first television appearance on *The Ed Sullivan Show* on Sunday night are seeping though and show fantastic results.

First estimates of 30,000,000 have now gone completely by the board, and experts inform me that upwards of 60,000,000 people throughout the United States watched the Sullivan show – more than the programme has ever had before, even with Elvis Presley in it at his peak.

A TICKET TO RIDE

PASSING THE TIME: John conducts an interview on the train while Ringo signs an autograph

CROWDED PLATFORM: Paul has trouble getting off the train when The Beatles arrived in Washington DC

I say, chaps, it's The Beatles!

WEDNESDAY, FEBRUARY 12 – It was snowing when The Beatles arrived by train in Washington from New York yesterday. But they got a warm welcome from 300 fans – most of them schoolgirls.

Because of the snow The Beatles were unable to fly in. That's why they made the four-hour train trip.

Because of the snow the girls were let out of classes early. They made a bee-line for the station carrying mock-English banners reading 'Welcome to The Beatles. A jolly good group, what!'

A solid wall of policemen kept enough order for drummer Ringo – star of this fabulously successful tour – to hold an informal fan-club conference on the station.

The Beatles were on their way to a double-date in the American capital: A concert at the 8,000-seat Coliseum theatre is a complete sell-out, while a ball in aid of charity and organised by the British Embassy follows.

PACKING UP: *Ringo's drum kit is dismantled by road manager Mal Evans after a sensational show at the Coliseum in Washington*

SISTER ACT: *George catches up with his sister Louise while in Washington*

Scoring a diplomatic triumph at the Embassy

FRIDAY, FEBRUARY 14 – The Beatles were guests of honour at a ball in the British Embassy, Washington. During this diplomatic triumph, one top lady produced a pair of scissors and snipped off a lock of Ringo Starr's hair.

Most of the time the lads found themselves signing autographs for dinner-jacketed diplomats and their fashionably gowned wives. One of their ardent fans was their hostess, Ambassador's wife Lady Ormsby-Gore.

SURROUNDED: *Even at a formal affair at the British Embassy there was no escaping the crowds for Paul*

THE LOST TOUR DIARY

A crowd even Churchill couldn't match

The Beatles gave their most electrifying performance of their careers before a screaming, yelling audience at the Coliseum, Washington, last night.

Then they went on to a charity dance at the British Embassy where Ringo asked the Ambassador (Sir David Ormsby-Gore) "What exactly do you do?"

They told me in the early hours of this morning at the British Embassy: "We've never had such a big crowd as this for any affair – not even when Sir Winston Churchill came."

The Beatles were there as guests, and what started out as a charity dance arranged by Lady Ormsby-Gore, wife of the

British Ambassador, for Embassy staff and friends, blossomed into Washington's most popular social engagement.

John, Paul, George and Ringo performed before 8,000 ecstatic fans in the vast ice stadium here called the Coliseum. Their stage looked like a boxing ring without ropes in the centre, and the audience was all round them.

But what an audience. Some fainted in the excitement and required the attention of ambulancemen.

John Lennon and Paul McCartney both gasped afterwards: "Weren't they great out there?" George Harrison, wiping his brow, just said: "Fabulous."

Jelly babies were showered at them – because they were once foolish enough to mention that they like those things.

One cop said to me, knowing I was English: "Call off your Beatles. Washington surrenders."

CARNEGIE BALL: A billboard announces the arrival of The Beatles

> 'It was one of the most extraordinary things I've seen. I loved it. They were marvellous. They have a lot of talent'

Smuggled in through a food lift

Later today Liverpool's chirpy Beatles bid adieu to New York and fly to Miami Beach, Florida, for the final stage of their American tour.

Behind them in New York they are leaving – sighing with relief – 500 policemen and security guards who, for the first time in six days, will be able to return to the peace and quiet of their everyday jobs.

They will be dealing with gunmen, kidnappers, robbers and dope peddlers instead of trying to hold in check a few thousand teenage girls guilty of Beatles worship.

Mrs Nelson Rockefeller, wife of New York's millionaire governor, was at one of the Carnegie Hall concerts with her 10-year-old daughter, Wendy.

She told reporters afterwards: "It was one of the most extraordinary things I've seen. I loved it. They were marvellous. They have a lot of talent."

BEATLE FEVER: The boys play at Carnegie Hall

"I like your dad's centre," said George Harrison.

Getting The Beatles to the hall was a problem. They were put in the food lift, rushed through the kitchens, out of the employees' entrance and up some steps to three waiting taxis.

HITTING THE RIGHT KEYS IN
FLORIDA
Boys mix business and pleasure in Miami

WE ARE SAILING:
Some relaxation
time aboard a
93-foot yacht

A reception beyond the boys' wildest dreams

I came an hour ahead of the Beatles from New York to see what, if anything, was being prepared for their arrival. It shook me when I walked off the plane to find every viewing spot at the vast airport packed with teenagers, mostly schoolgirls.

Many carried huge posters blaring 'We love you, Beatles'. They had a four-page local newspaper supplement devoted entirely to the boys.

It was the biggest turnout I've seen anywhere since we arrived in America. At least 8,000 youngsters was the estimate of airport officials – more than for any other visitor in Miami records.

Girls screamed, squealed and swarmed everywhere, stopping all traffic leaving and approaching the airport. Many incoming would-be passengers missed their plane through being caught in the snarl.

When the Beatles slipped away from the tarmac in a car with a police escort, leaving thousands of beat chicks unaware that they had gone, trouble began among them, leading to broken windows, chairs and other furniture.

John Lennon said: "We never dreamed of a reception like this. Getting down here in Florida, more than a thousand miles from New York, we really thought they'd not be too bothered about us. But this lot are just fabulous – bigger than in New York."

THE LOST TOUR DIARY

Police accuse radio stations of 'stirring kids up'

While the carefree, multi-million dollar-earners The Beatles are lazing in the sunshine aboard a sleek cabin-cruiser far off-shore, the shaken city of Miami is busy totting up in hard cash the cost to the ratepayers of their tumultuous reception by 8,000 frenzied fans.

Police chief Jesse Barkett estimated: "The ratepayers will foot a bill for nearly $1,500 (£500) for the services of extra policemen who had to be taken off other jobs to reinforce the airport police."

Two local radio stations, which have plugged The Beatles' records hard in the last few weeks and called on teenage listeners to welcome The Beatles, were accused by the police

of being responsible for building up hysteria among youngsters, thus creating the airport havoc.

"This wouldn't have happened if those radio stations hadn't stirred the kids up," declared Chief Barkett.

Paul, Ringo and George, wearing brand new Miami-style white t-shirts, yarned with me in their suite.

I asked them what had been the greatest experience of their American tour.

Ringo Starr replied: "No doubt at all. Coming here – this fabulous Miami beach."

George Harrison, now completely recovered from his throat infection, waved a hand in the direction of the blue Atlantic, lapping directly beneath their balcony window on the 12th floor of the luxury Deauville ▶

MAKING A SPLASH: Even during a paddle in the sea off Miami Beach female attention isn't far away

THE WATER BEATLES RELAX

SATURDAY, FEBRUARY 15 – The Beatles went on a five-hour yacht trip yesterday – and got away from the crowds that have been following them everywhere in Miami, Florida.

They went aboard the 93-ft pleasure craft Southern Trail, owned by furniture millionaire Bernard Castro.

John Lennon and Paul McCartney wore yachting caps. It was shorts and t-shirts for Ringo Starr and George Harrison.

Said John: "We want to be alone." And Ringo: "Away from everybody."

They had hoped for a quiet holiday in Miami. But their fantastic success in America has made this almost impossible.

The Beatles were due to return to Britain a few days later but with snow, sleet and fog enveloping London, they decided to stay in sunny Miami until the following weekend.

'They had hoped for a quiet holiday but their fantastic success has made this almost impossible'

SUN AND SEA: John in relaxed mood during a five-hour sailing trip

Hotel, and said: "You see this place on TV and movies at home but you can't imagine what it's like until you get here.

"We had a picture of New York in our minds' eye before we arrived and what we saw there wasn't any different from what we had imagined.

"But this Miami has kicked us sideways. We never dreamed anywhere could be so marvellous."

Paul McCartney grinned and commented: "Fancy having breakfast in the sunshine on your hotel balcony. This is even better than New Brighton."

They all agreed that the Americans' reception in New York, Washington and here far exceeded their widest imaginings.

Said Ringo: "We thought before we got here, you know, that America has everything and we didn't know how they'd take us.

"When we reached New York we knew everything was going to be okay. From that moment we've felt on top of the world."

Extended holiday

The mop-headed Beatles originally planned to return to England around now.

But after a second appearance on the Ed Sullivan television show, the boys announced their intention of staying at Miami Beach a few days longer.

"If we weren't booked to appear on television in England next weekend, we would probably have stayed even longer," declared Paul McCartney.

The Beatles extended their stay in Florida strictly for relaxation after their strenuous tour. Despite many immensely tempting propositions, they are doing no more shows.

Last night's television show brought the usual teenage riots outside the hotel, but the audience at the performance had an average age of at least 30.

The elderly audience, who had not done anything to get seats except stay at the correct hotels, looked askance at them.

Ringo Starr said to me afterwards: "The audience was dead. We only heard a few chicks yelling from the back rows. It was dismal."

Yet from outside, the nationwide audience voted The Beatles a tremendous success.

THE LOST TOUR DIARY

A very big bang in American show business

The *New York Times*, the most staid and highly respected newspaper in America, yesterday devoted a whole page to analysing the reason for Beatlemania.

'In nine days in this country The Beatles have made a deep impression on the American sub-culture,' the article observes.

'They can look with gratification at the dominance of the Liverpool sound on those American radio stations consecrated day and night to rock 'n' roll, at skyrocketing sales of their records, at the thriving trade in Beatles' products of all kinds.'

The quartet expect to return to the United States in August after their tour of Australia in June, Brian Epstein told me today.

Just about everybody who's

had anything to do with the Beatles' American adventure agrees that the fuse which fired the rocket in this country was signing for three appearances on the Ed Sullivan show.

Three consecutive weeks of topping the programme – Brian Epstein insisted that The Beatles received top billing throughout – means they are making a very big bang in American show business.

This month the three biggest national magazines are displaying The Beatles on their covers.

Almost unknown in the United States five weeks ago, The Beatles brought Ed Sullivan the biggest rating in television history, and when we leave here, the boys will have earned nearly £100,000 from their appearances plus royalties on records sold in one month.

I, Cassius Clay, say those Beatles are ok

WEDNESDAY, FEBRUARY 19 – It was quite a beat-up when five of the world's biggest money-spinning 'mouths' got together in a beach gymnasium here.

Boxer Cassius Clay, otherwise known as the Louisville Lip, beat his chest in triumph after flooring the four Beatles, who mouth the Mersey Beat to the tune of millions.

Cassius, shrewd showman that he is, grabbed the limelight from the moment he walked into the gym where he is training for his world heavyweight title fight with champion Sonny Liston.

The Beatles had been hanging around for some time before Cassius walked into the gym shouting: "Where are the Beatles?"

Beatle George had been getting very restless. He had threatened to walk out unless the challenger put in a quick appearance.

Cassius grabbed the limelight from the moment the five stepped into the ring.

He picked up Ringo at one point and waved him around at the crowd.

Then he got The Beatles to lie at his feet. Tied to his wrist was a disc bearing the inscription 'Stamp out the Beatles'.

Magnanimously, Clay paid a tribute to the Beatles at the end of their meeting.

He said: "They must be great because they have the world all shook up and I'm the greatest."

DAILY MIRROR, Wednesday, February 19, 1964   PAGE 13

Presenting—on your left—the Louisville Lip .. and on your right, George, Ringo, John and Paul

I, CASSIUS CLAY, SAY THOSE BEATLES ARE OK

From BARRIE HARDING, Miami, Florida, Tuesday

IT was quite a beat-up when five of the world's biggest money-spinning "mouths" got together in a beach gymnasium here today.

Boxer Cassius Clay, otherwise known as the Louisville Lip, beat his chest, in triumph after flooring the four Beatles, who mouth the Mersey Beat to the tune of millions.

Cassius, shrewd showman that he is, grabbed the limelight from the moment he walked into the gym where he is training for his world heavyweight title fight with champion Sonny Liston.

Restless

The Beatles—John Lennon, Paul McCartney, George Harrison and Ringo Starr—had been hanging around for some time before Cassius walked into the gym shouting: "Where are the Beatles?"

Beatle George had been getting very restless. He had threatened to walk out unless the challenger put in a quick appearance.

Cassius grabbed the limelight from the moment the five stepped into the ring.

He stuck cards that were conveniently ready into the hands of the Beatles and got them to hold them aloft.

The cards said simply: "Six foot three, 216lb—the greatest."

It was probably the zaniest session ever seen in a boxing gymnasium.

A big hand from Cassius "sends" Beatles George Harrison, Ringo Starr, John Lennon and Paul McCartney.

Enter Sir Alec, in the role of the happy father

By SUSAN CURTIS-BENNETT

AFFAIRS of State were pushed into the background for a few minutes at No. 10, Downing-street, yesterday.

They were overshadowed by an Affair of the Heart.

Meriel Douglas-Home, the Prime Minister's guitar-playing daughter, sat in the green and gold drawing-room with her fiance, Oxford don Adrian Darby.

As her mother, Lady Douglas-Home, arranged flowers, into the room stepped Sir Alec.

AIRPORT READY FOR FAN INVASION

FRIDAY, FEBRUARY 21 – At 7.40 tomorrow morning the Beatles will arrive back at London Airport.

Airport officials were getting ready to cope with the crowds of fans who are planning a giant 'welcome home' for the group.

A spokesman said: "We are preparing for the biggest-ever turnout of Beatle fans."

The jet bringing The Beatles home is being switched from the usual long distance arrival runway.

It will taxi up to No. 1 passenger building and the Queen's building.

This has been done so that fans can get a good view of The Beatles from the roof terrace of the two buildings.

While they wait, Beatles records will be played over the roof gardens public address system.

MEN IN WHITE: The four lads strike a relaxed pose during their stay in Miami

Cynthia bemused by boys' visit to Clay's gym

While smiling photographers, reporters and fight fans scrambled madly on to the apron of the boxing ring to watch The Beatles fooling around with Cassius Clay, one quiet woman stayed in the background a few feet away, practically unnoticed.

Cynthia, the lovely blonde wife of John Lennon, stood by my side, looking with bewilderment at the seething mass around the ringside.

This gymnasium on Fifth Street, Miami Beach, where Clay is training for next Tuesday's world title crack at Sonny Liston – is tatty, dirty and sweaty, with the smell of liniment everywhere.

Poor Cynthia Lennon looked a little child lost in a forest full of giant ogres.

She whispered to me: "I've never seen anything like this in my life. They told John that there wouldn't be anybody here except Cassius Clay and a few photographers, or I wouldn't have come."

Cassius Clay made the most of The Beatles' visit. Pausing for a few moments amid his clowning, he composed this breathtaking piece of poetry about the occasion:

"When Liston reads about The Beatles visiting me,
He'll get so mad, I'll knock him out in three."

What did The Beatles think of talkative Cassius?

Ringo Starr shrugged and said: "He's big but gentle. He shook my hand and I still have the use of three fingers."

George Harrison said: "I've got no interest in the fight game."

Paul McCartney said: "It's a bit of a giggle, isn't it?"

John Lennon commented: "Let's get out of here and get some sun."

THE LOST TOUR DIARY

'Your Beatles make our girls act like crazy'

Teenage fans went to astonishing lengths last night to try to sneak through the cordon of police and security guards surrounding the Deauville Hotel.

There, Liverpool's suntanned Beatles were busy packing in readiness for today's reluctant farewell to Miami Beach.

Police told me two girls were found sleeping under tables in the hotel kitchen at an early hour. They had got in by posing as cleaners.

Three schoolgirl beat-chicks were discovered well after midnight trying to climb a fire escape which they thought might lead them to the 12th floor, where The Beatles' apartments are situated.

Police have played a continual game of hide and seek with girls running through the hotel basement and service entrances.

Wiping his sweating brow, one officer, revolver on hip, said to me: "Don't get me wrong, sir, but we gonna be mighty glad when your Beatles get out of here. They're good lads, but they sure got something that makes our girls act like crazy."

Beatlemania reigns supreme as we leave for New York, then on to London.

HOMECOMING HEROES

LOUD AND PROUD: Fans camp out to welcome The Beatles back to England while the boys themselves are clearly impressed with the turnout

Fans camp out to show their pride as The Beatles return

SATURDAY, FEBRUARY 22 – The Beatles were flying home...and building up all through last night was the greatest "welcome home" London Airport has ever seen.

By 2am this morning, bewildered airport police were trying to calm down 1,000 worshipping fans.

They were amazing scenes as the girls chanted "Beatle, Beatle, Beatle."

They waved Beatle pictures, Beatle banners, Beatle hats – even a "Welcome Home Beatles" banner made from daffodils.

Winter holidaymakers and tourists stared open-mouthed at the carnival on the main building's carpeted balcony as the girls sang The Beatles' hit songs.

One policeman mopped his brow and said: "Blimey, I've never seen a show like this – and The Beatles aren't even here yet."

The balcony was like a giant camp. Girls stretched out on the carpet talking of nothing but Ringo, John, Paul and George.

And police were told to prepare for 11 coach-loads of fans from Liverpool, and another 16 coaches from the Midlands and the south.

The night wore on. Still the fans came, and at least 6,000 teenagers were expected to turn up for breakfast-time with The Beatles.

The gathering of the fans had begun shortly before midnight, then a steady stream turned the second floor of the main passenger terminal into a 'refugee camp'.

Blankets were unrolled, food parcels unpacked, and transistor radios blared above the babble of voices.

Police, accompanied by searching parents, went among the 'refugees' looking for local girls. Some tried to find hideouts in the airport, but many had come too far to go home.

They carried banners reading 'Welcome home Beatles' and 'Beatles you have done Britain proud'.

The Beatles began their journey home last night by flying from Miami to New York's Kennedy International Airport where they changed planes.

As the Miami plane landed, airport workers stood by with fire hoses and 180 policemen forced back a screaming crowd of 4,000 teenagers.

When The Beatles appeared at the top of the plane steps, the teenagers let out a fantastic roar.

It grew to a crescendo as they walked to the London plane, which had been renamed from 'Defiant' to 'The Beatles'.

Blinking in the harsh glare of film and television arc lamps, they climbed the ramp.

George Harrison put his hands above his head in a boxer's salute and the other Beatles joined in. Laughing, they waved to the crowd and said: "Thank you, we'll be back."

RAPTUROUS RECEPTION:
The Beatles left behind one set of ecstatic fans in America to be greeted by another set when they returned to England

THE BEATLES'
US NUMBER ONE
HIT SINGLES

I WANT TO HOLD YOUR HAND
FEB 1ST 1964 (7 WEEKS)

SHE LOVES YOU
MAR 21ST 1964 (2 WEEKS)

CAN'T BUY ME LOVE
APR 4TH 1964 (5 WEEKS)

LOVE ME DO
MAY 30TH 1964 (1 WEEK)

HARD DAY'S NIGHT
AUG 1ST 1964 (2 WEEKS)

I FEEL FINE
DEC 26TH 1964 (3 WEEKS)

EIGHT DAYS A WEEK
MAR 13TH 1965 (2 WEEKS)

TICKET TO RIDE
MAY 22ND 1965 (1 WEEK)

HELP!
SEP 4TH 1965 (3 WEEKS)

YESTERDAY
OCT 9TH 1965 (4 WEEKS)

WE CAN WORK IT OUT
JAN 8TH 1966 (3 WEEKS)

PAPERBACK WRITER
JUN 25TH 1966 (2 WEEKS)

PENNY LANE
MAR 18TH 1967 (1 WEEK)

ALL YOU NEED IS LOVE
AUG 19TH 1967 (1 WEEK)

HELLO GOODBYE
DEC 30TH 1967 (3 WEEKS)

HEY JUDE
SEP 28TH 1968 (9 WEEKS)

GET BACK
MAY 24TH 1969 (5 WEEKS)

COME TOGETHER/SOMETHING
NOV 29TH 1969 (1 WEEK)

LET IT BE
APR 11TH 1970 (2 WEEKS)

THE LONG AND WINDING ROAD
JUN 13TH 1970 (2 WEEKS)

BACK IN THE US of A

After the success of their first tour, the boys return to San Francisco six months later for a second dose of American-style Beatlemania

THE BEATLES IN THE USA/CANADA, SUMMER 1964

August 19: Cow Palace, San Francisco
August 20: Convention Hall, Las Vegas
August 21: Seattle Center, Seattle
August 22: Empire Stadium, Vancouver
August 23: Hollywood Bowl, Los Angeles
August 26: Red Rocks Amphitheatre, Denver
August 27: Cincinnati Gardens, Cincinnati
August 28: Forest Hills, New York City
August 29: Forest Hills, New York City
August 30: Convention Hall, Atlantic City
September 2: Convention Hall, Philadelphia
September 3: Indiana State Fair Coliseum, Indianapolis
September 4: Milwaukee Arena, Milwaukee
September 5: International Amphitheatre, Chicago
September 6: Olympia Stadium, Detroit
September 7: Maple Leaf Gardens, Toronto
September 8: Montreal Forum, Montreal
September 11: Gator Bowl Stadium, Jacksonville
September 12: Boston Garden, Boston
September 13: Baltimore Civic Center, Baltimore
September 14: Civic Arena, Pittsburgh
September 15: Public Auditorium, Cleveland
September 16: City Park Stadium, New Orleans
September 17: Municipal Stadium, Kansas City
September 18: Memorial Auditorium, Dallas
September 20: Paramount Theater, New York City

Minimising the dangers of mass hysteria

Teenage girls were knocked down and trampled on, and young children had to be snatched into the arms of police to save them from serious injury when 10,000 fans erupted into a frenzy in San Francisco on the arrival of Liverpool's Beatles to start their American-Canadian tour.

It was one of the most frightening examples of how mob enthusiasm can bring near disaster I have ever seen. Only tremendous work by an army of police under Sheriff Earl Whitmore and a quick getaway from the scene by John, Paul, George and Ringo prevented a heavy accident toll.

To gain some control over the huge crowd expected at the airport, officials decided to erect wire barricades nearly a mile from the normal air landing terminal. The fans were told if they remained inside the corral and didn't break the barriers when The Beatles arrived, the boys would appear on a platform in the centre of the enclosure, and speak over microphones.

The emotional build-up, fanned by blazing heat, was brought to a climax by the sight of The Beatles' limousine. In seconds, the car was brought to a halt by a screaming, fighting mass of many hundreds of girls crowding round banging the windows, doors and jumping on the bonnet.

Police managed to force a path through by sheer muscle power for The Beatles to reach the platform where briefly they said how pleased they were to be in California.

Then as the girls broke through the barriers and approached the platform, manager Brian Epstein gave the thumbs down signal to the boys, indicating 'get away – it's getting dangerous.'

Immediately, Paul, John, George and Ringo leaped from the platform and jumped into a waiting car, which swept off so swiftly very few fans realised what was happening. When they did, there was one mad rush for the exit through which The Beatles' car had disappeared.

OVERCOME WITH EXHAUSTION: Fans are attended to by the authorities after screaming their greetings to The Beatles near San Francisco Airport
LEFT: The aftermath of a frantic occasion

'POSSE' TO PROTECT BEATLES

TUESDAY, AUGUST 18 – A sheriff's posse will hustle The Beatles inside a specially built wire fence when they fly in to San Francisco today.

The aim: To avoid complete chaos when the fans – well over 50,000 are expected – scream their welcome at the start of The Beatles' tour.

The Beatles' paddock has been built in a field nearly a mile from the main airport terminal.

Paul, John, Ringo and George will appear on a 3ft. platform for the fans.

Beatle suite invaded by girls after frenzied airport welcome

THURSDAY, AUGUST 20 – A mob of girls invaded The Beatles' hotel suite in San Francisco yesterday.

The girls – about 40 of them – surprised and overran a cordon of guards, and rushed for The Beatles' rooms.

But the guards beat them to it, shoved them into lifts and turned them out of the luxury Hilton Hotel where The Beatles are staying at

SAFE SPOT: John, Paul, George and Ringo meet their San Francisco fans

the start of their second tour of America.

The girls got to The Beatles' floor by creeping up 15 flights of stairs. They made their final rush through fire-escape doors.

At San Francisco airport The Beatles flew in to a welcome by 10,000 frenzied girls.

The band went in a steel-mesh pen specially built so they could meet their fans in safety.

Under the pressure of young bodies, the steel uprights of the fence began to bend. Cracks appeared in the concrete in which they were sunk. The Beatles were whipped out of the corral and into their car.

'The girls – about 40 of them – overran a cordon of guards and rushed for The Beatles' rooms'

FLYAWAY BEATLES FOOL 16,000 FANS

FRIDAY, AUGUST 21 – The Beatles flew into Las Vegas for the second concert of their American tour after being smuggled out of San Francisco...with the help of a white lie and a decoy car.

The white lie was told to 16,000 exhausted fans at the end of The Beatles' opening show at the Cow Palace, San Francisco. The lie: That The Beatles were hurrying back to their hotel at once.

The car was driven away from the Palace to fool the fans' scouts waiting outside the dressing room.

An hour later The Beatles made a secret rendezvous at San Francisco airport and boarded a specially chartered plane for Las Vegas.

It had been a hard day's night. On top of the usual hysterics, The Beatles had to face a barrage of jelly beans from the Cow Palace audience.

And jelly beans are harder missiles than the English jelly babies.

After two warnings that The Beatles would quit if any more beans were thrown, the barrage stopped.

One of the countless visitors to The Beatles' dressing room was Shirley Temple – a Hollywood child star before the Liverpool lads were born.

Despite the frantic scenes only two youths were injured at Cow Palace. But at an empty Las Vegan airport the police took no chances.

With truncheons drawn and led by a deputy sheriff who had a snarling Alsatian on a lead, they escorted The Beatles to the Sahara Hotel.

The police needn't have bothered. Hundreds of gamblers there were apparently unaware that the VIP guests had arrived.

Later things warmed up when scores of suntanned girls invaded the hotel corridors in search of their idols.

QUICK GETAWAY: The Fab Four perform at the Cow Palace in San Francisco before being whisked off to an airplane bound for Las Vegas while (right) the lads carry on regardless at another gig as one unconscious fan is carried away

THE LOST TOUR DIARY

Midnight getaway to catch Nevada flight

My prediction that The Beatles would slip out of San Francisco after their show last night and head for Las Vegas has come off.

Brian Epstein left the decision to the boys whether to fly to Nevada's fabulous gambling Mecca immediately after their performance or spend another night in San Francisco.

They promptly decided to make a midnight flit in our private charter plane, while 16,000 ecstatic fans still milled around the Cow Palace crying: "We want The Beatles."

Two Beatles went out together from the hotel in the early hours of our last day in San Francisco.

Ringo and John learned that Billy Preston, with whom they appeared on a number of occasions in Germany, New Brighton and elsewhere, was playing with his own group at a nightclub in San Francisco's Chinatown.

About 3am they decided to spend a couple of happy hours with him before returning to the hotel without being troubled.

'After two warnings that The Beatles would quit if any more jelly beans were thrown, the barrage stopped'

SWEET MOMENT: *The Cow Palace performance was interrupted by over-enthusiastic fans throwing jelly beans*

A SUREFIRE WINNER IN VEGAS

THE LOST TOUR DIARY

No gamble on safety as boys stay locked up!

With a blazing sun desert rocketing the temperature into the mid-90s and the Sahara Hotel's two swimming pools beckoning invitingly, our bouncing Beatles are still wandering idly around their rooms on the 47th floor.

It is not their fault, mind you. Manager Brian Epstein explained: "The hotel management requested the boys not to use the public gaming rooms because their presence would attract large numbers of young fans."

The laws here prohibit anyone under the age of 21 being in the casino. Hotel officials feared that the presence of the boys would cause an influx of teenagers.

John, Paul, George and Ringo weren't too happy about it, but accepted the restriction of their movements with the proviso that they be allowed to explore the exciting city after they had finished their two shows.

Ringo said to me: "What's the fun of being in Las Vegas without going out at night."

For the benefit of photographers, two one-armed bandits were borrowed from the hotel and humped into a bedroom where The Beatles were pictured expressing delight and sorrow in order as they pulled the handles. It seems a shame to prick the bubbles but the machines had been fixed so that they didn't take in or pay out any cash.

John Lennon was reluctant to figure in pictures and for a long time just watched the others.

"I think gambling's all wrong. Why encourage it?" he said sternly to pressmen. Eventually he gave in and joined the others.

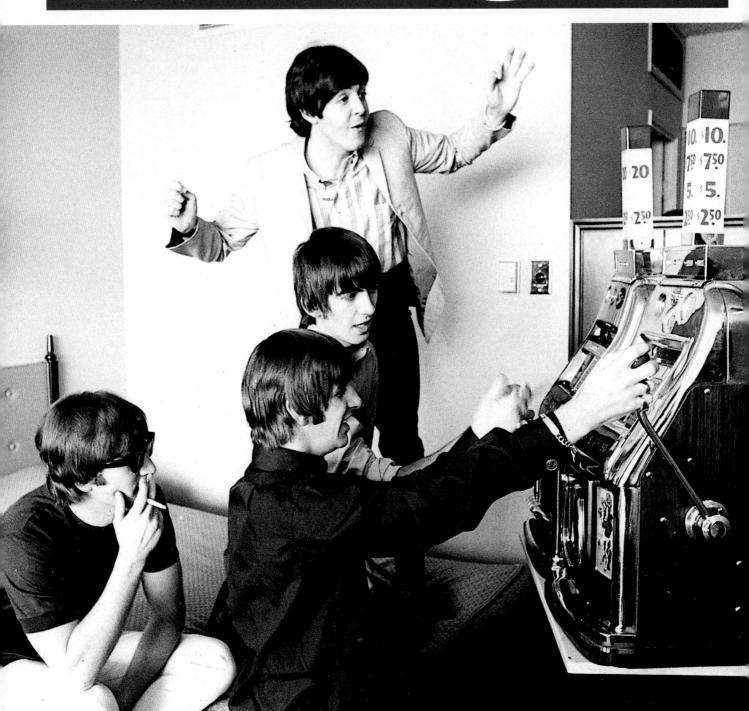

LUCKY STREAK: John looks on as Ringo, George and Paul play a slot machine that was brought up to their room in the Sahara Hotel

GAMBLERS' PARADISE WELCOMES ITS BIGGEST EVER ACT

SATURDAY, AUGUST 22 – They had singer Pat Boone swinging in the aisle. Liberace got the beat.

And a burly sheriff's deputy, his gun firmly in his holster, took a blind girl gently by the hand and put her in a front seat to hear *I Want To Hold Your Hand*.

The Beatles from Liverpool had finally arrived in Las Vegas – the American showtown which pays more famous artists more money for stage appearances than any other entertainment centre in the world.

Stan Irwin, the wealthy showman who arranged their appearance here, introduced them as the biggest act ever to come to this giant gambling city in the state of Nevada.

For The Beatles this was a show different from any other they had given in any other part of the world.

One-third of the audience were mothers and fathers. From all over the West these parents brought their daughters to Las Vegas to hear The Beatles.

As gamblers, none of the four Beatles could be described as the last of the big spenders.

When three of them posed for a picture with a one-armed bandit, John Lennon said: "I think gambling is evil, so why should I encourage it?"

This must have sounded like sheer treason to the big wheels of this big-spending city.

STRONG CAST:
John, Paul, George
and Ringo go
fishing from their
hotel room in The
Edgewater, Seattle

SEA FISHING *in* SEATTLE

Washington trip gives awesome foursome a chance to relax

TUESDAY, AUGUST 25 – These four young men lead a whirlwind life.

They fly around the world, and hardly get a chance to take a really good look at it.

But now, at last, they have managed to snatch a few moments' peace. Away from the screaming fans and the hullabaloo of their hectic American tour...The Beatles have gone fishin'.

It was how Britain's beat ambassadors spent a few hours relaxing in Seattle, Washington.

It just so happened that their hotel window overlooked a stretch of water. So out came the fishing rods.

But it was a hard day's wait. They didn't get a bite.

RING OF STEEL: Security levels are high as The Beatles play to a packed out Seattle Center

Sheriff's men make late-night room invasion

The Beatles left Las Vegas yesterday for the 1,000 miles to Seattle after a sleepless night.

They were disturbed in the early hours by revolver-armed sheriff's men knocking them up and demanding admission.

Reports had gone anonymously to police headquarters that teenagers were in The Beatles' bedrooms. Officials had to act. For these fictitious under-age girls, they searched the rooms.

John, Paul, George and Ringo were rudely awakened by door banging and stood yawning in their pyjamas as hard-faced officials looked around the rooms, and then went out apologising "for any inconvenience we have caused you".

Hoax helps boys escape

A screaming crowd of teenagers trapped The Beatles in their dressing room at the Seattle Coliseum last night.

The Beatles had appeared for 29 minutes, during which time the stage was peppered with jelly beans and peanuts. The noise of the packed house of 14,000 drowned the music.

When the Merseysiders left the stage, a group of about 20 teenagers charged towards them, but police managed to throw up a cordon long enough to get the group in their dressing room.

When they tried to leave the Coliseum, their car was mobbed and they were escorted back to their dressing room.

Time after time, hysterical youngsters fought to break through lines of police and sailors, while officials sought ways to get The Beatles out of the building.

Finally, after an hour, an ambulance was backed into a dark alley in the building, a group of sailors climbed in and The Beatles crawled in among them. A crowd of about 200 howled when they learned they had been hoaxed.

The STARS of HOLLYWOOD

The rich and famous of Beverly Hills queue up for exclusive access

WEDNESDAY, AUGUST 26 – It was all going to be so sophisticated when the Beatles put in an appearance at a children's party in Beverly Hills.

For the young guests – at £9 a time for charity – were the celebrity-proof children of Hollywood's famous film stars.

But it didn't quite work out as planned.

The 'scream-proof' children made a dash to touch George Harrison, Paul McCartney, Ringo Starr and John Lennon when they arrived at the exclusive garden party.

And the four Liverpool beat boys – currently on a tour of America – were besieged by children with stars trailing after their very excited youngsters.

Among the famous parents were Lloyd Bridges, Hedda Hoppa and the lovely Eva Marie Saint.

Shelley Winters, who went along with her daughter Vittoria, was herself a victim of Beatlemania.

She announced: "We have just touched a Beatle, and we'll never wash our hands again."

GARDEN PARTY: Children of the rich and famous enjoy a meeting with The Beatles in Beverly Hills

'The guests were the celebrity-proof children of Hollywood's famous film stars. But it didn't quite work out as planned'

'Twice as many
girls squeal
for Ringo in
America as
for the other
three Beatles
combined'

RINGO IS THE BIG DRAW IN AMERICA

THURSDAY, AUGUST 27 – In an airliner somewhere above the Rocky Mountains, a millionaire barely out of his teens was reading an old magazine article which asked: 'Are the Beatles finished?'

Paul McCartney can be excused a smile of amusement.

For he and his three fellow Beatles are now a quarter of the way through an amazing tour which is making showbiz history.

In one city alone they are being paid nearly £80,000 for 40 minutes' work.

Some estimates here put their earnings for the four-week tour at three-quarters of a million pounds.

And while they do their stage act in the big arenas of America, hundreds of thousands of dollars are cascading into the box offices of cinemas showing their film *A Hard Day's Night*.

In a country where everything is big, even the Americans are gasping at the enormity of the Merseyside group's success.

Life magazine tried to explain it in a front cover and six pages of pictures and articles this week.

The *Miami Herald* went all hysterical one morning with six text-sized pages of pictures and articles.

But what has really stunned this country is the intensity of the emotions the Beatles drag out of America's young maidens.

When this tour ends, one young man, Ringo Starr, will never be quite the same again.

Once the shy, reserved member of the group, he has now blossomed into a striking personality.

Twice as many girls squeal for Ringo here as for the other three Beatles combined.

COWBOYS AND ENGLISHMEN: *The boys get the chance to play at being cowboys at a ranch near Bel Air during their time in Los Angeles*

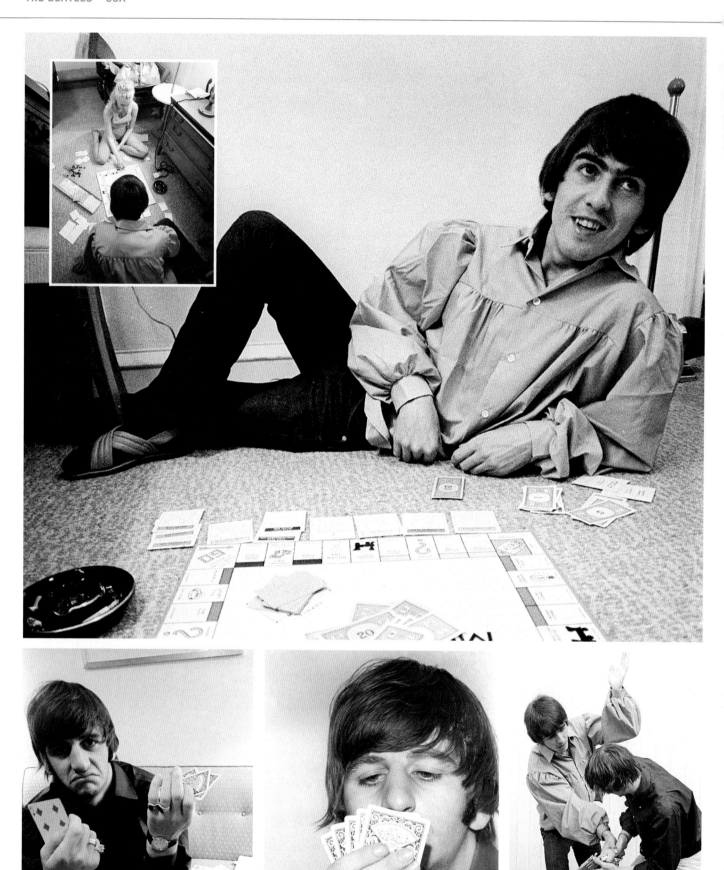

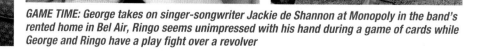
GAME TIME: George takes on singer-songwriter Jackie de Shannon at Monopoly in the band's rented home in Bel Air, Ringo seems unimpressed with his hand during a game of cards while George and Ringo have a play fight over a revolver

CHANCE TO CHILL OUT: The lads lark around by the pool at their Bel Air apartment where Paul almost went for an unplanned dip in the water

THE LOST TOUR DIARY

Airplane unrest as fans implore boys not to fly

In our aircraft today as we leave Hollywood for Denver, Colorado, there's a strange air of unrest.

A woman called Mrs Jeane Dixon has allegedly made a forecast of doom ahead of our private charter flight and some members of the supporting company who are accompanying us on this package tour are getting worried.

Mrs Dixon is supposed to be able to foretell the future.

It is said here that she predicted the assassination of President Kennedy and the death in an air-crash of Dag Hammerskjold, the United Nations' former secretary-general.

It was George Harrison who told me that this woman had

forecast our plane would crash on the 900-mile flight between Philadelphia and Indianapolis, where the Beatles are booked to appear on September 3.

George said: "Before we left England we had letters from hundreds of fans in America, pleading with us not to fly to Indianapolis. They seemed silly to us. Who's this woman anyway? Why do people listen and even pay attention to such rubbish? Yet they do, obviously. We have got £1,000,000 life insurance on this trip, anyway."

Paul McCartney's comment was: "Anyone who believes in that kind of stuff believes in ghosts and spirits. It's nutty."

I've discovered that Mrs Dixon never did make this prophecy.

She admits making other forecasts which proved unhappily true, but says: "I've never mentioned a Beatles plane disaster and I cannot understand why this thing has flared up."

BIG RECEPTION
in the
BIG APPLE

FOUR ACES: The boys perform at the Forest Hills Tennis Stadium in New York

POPPING BY: Bob Dylan waits for his first meeting with The Beatles. He would famously introduce them to marijuana

MESSAGE OF LOVE: One fan hopes to get Ringo's attention

THE LOST TOUR DIARY

Backstage thief takes camera, shirts and rings

The Beatles arrived in New York, thrilled with the reception from 15,000 deliriously happy fans at last night's show in Cincinnati.

But they are angry that "just about the greatest night of the tour," as John Lennon described it, should have been spoiled by backstage thieves who stole personal articles and even gifts from fans out of their dressing room while everyone was occupied on stage.

Mal Evans, the road manager, was the principal sufferer from the thieves.

Evans lost a camera taken from a bag on a table in The Beatles' dressing room.

He told me on the plane from Cincinnati to New York, where the boys have shows tonight and tomorrow: "It's been impossible so far to list what's been stolen, but certainly a dozen of the stage dress shirts which the boys use have gone, plus a few hundred cigarettes, many rings sent in by fans to Ringo, and other gifts. It happened when the boys went on stage for their act."

Ringo gets his lost medal back

SATURDAY, AUGUST 29 – The Beatles flew into Kennedy Airport from Cincinnati yesterday at 3.10am.

Three thousand screaming fans were at the airport barriers. The Beatles later got to their hotel to find more fans.

One frenzied 15-year-old flung her arms round Ringo to steal a kiss. When he broke free, his treasured St Christopher medallion had gone.

He had an appeal broadcast on radio. "The medallion means more to me than almost anything else," he said.

Ringo promised the girl who had the medallion a private meeting with The Beatles if she returned it. And 150 girls phoned to say they would take it back.

But later Angie McGowan, of New York, arrived with the medallion and said: "In the struggle, I thought I had a button in my hand. Later I discovered it was the medallion."

TOTALLY DEVOTED: *One young fan in New York uses a telescope to get a better view of his heroes while (right) this fan is in no doubt who her favourite is*

DEAFENING: *The streets of New York City were a crazy place to be when The Beatles came to town*

'Ringo promised the girl who had his medallion a private meeting with The Beatles if she returned it. 150 girls phoned to say they would take it back'

No segregation, insists McCartney

Paul McCartney's statement at a press conference that he and the rest of the Beatles would refuse to perform anywhere where segregation of white and black folk was allowed in the auditorium has brought a quick assurance from Jacksonville, Florida, where

the boys will perform in just over a week, that they have no segregation, nor any special section set apart from negroes.

A suggestion had in fact been made that Jacksonville intended imposing a form of colour bar which could 'pen' black members of the audience from others. The Beatles were angry at this information, but Paul told me tonight they were all delighted to hear that there would be no segregation in Jacksonville.

EERIE *in* INDIANA

Beatles are not in any danger claims psychic after rumours of Indianapolis death trip

WEDNESDAY, SEPTEMBER 2 – Crystal-gazer Jeane Dixon said yesterday: "Give the Beatles this message: It is safe for them to go to Indianapolis. They will not be in any danger."

Mrs Dixon, who predicted the death of President Kennedy, said reports that she had forecast that three Beatles would be killed in Indianapolis – where the party is due tonight – were "only rumours".

Some of the other acts in the American tour had asked to be allowed to travel separately.

Deputy tour boss Derek Taylor called Mrs Dixon himself to receive a personal assurance. "What a relief," he said. "Some of our people had been getting slightly unnerved."

SERVE AND PROTECT: John Lennon and the boys were rarely lonely as they visited the Indiana State Fair Coliseum

Record-breaking tour taking its physical toll

On the way back to the bank account of the Beatles goes another £85,000 as a result of last night's two magnificent shows in Indianapolis.

The whole of the state of Indiana annually makes a trek to Indianapolis for the gigantic State Fair.

The Beatles' visit was arranged neatly to come in the middle of the fair, with the result that more than 30,000 seats for their two performances were sold out at prices ranging up to 35 dollars per ticket. This tour is now obviously going to break all records for financial profit.

So far they have appeared in San Francisco, Las Vegas, Se-

attle, Vancouver, Los Angeles, Denver, Cincinnati, New York, Atlantic City, Philadelphia and now Indianapolis.

It's becoming a physical strain on all of us. John, Paul, George and Ringo did two shows last night before 30,000 screaming fans, without having had a wink of sleep for the previous 24 hours. All that time they had been either in their hotel or flying to and fro.

Now, just a footnote from Ringo Starr who asks me to wish his Mum and Dad a happy holiday when they take off tomorrow. So Richard and Elsie, back there in Admiral Grove, Dingle, Liverpool, your boy wishes you lots of sunshine and fun.

COP CODE FOR BEATLES FANS

THURSDAY, SEPTEMBER 3 – Police chief Alva Funk, who has obviously never seen The Beatles before, has issued a code of behaviour for the 26,000 fans who will be at the Liverpool boys' show today at the Indiana State Fair Coliseum.

The fans may: Scream, shout, cry hysterically, call out "Ringo", "Paul", "George" or "John" at intervals.

They may not: Meet the Beatles, collect

'Fans may scream, shout or cry hysterically. They may not get up from their seats during the performance'

EAR-SPLITTING:
This police officer doesn't seem to be enjoying the performance in Indiana as much as the fans sitting around him

autographs or get up from their seats during the performance.

In the Speedway Motel, next to the famous Indianapolis motor-racing circuit, where The Beatles are staying, 42 of the 96 rooms are occupied by cops.

Despite the precautions, a young fan slipped through the police net within 15 minutes of The Beatles' arrival. He got into their room – by carrying a waiter's tray.

THE LOST TOUR DIARY

Boys frustrated by too much protection

Angry because rigorous police security measures in many cities are preventing The Beatles from seeing or being seen by fans who wait many hours at airfields to welcome them, Paul McCartney has declared: "It's carrying protection to a ridiculous extent, and making us feel like heels."

Paul was acting as spokesman for The Beatles, who had just learned that their arrival later today in Chicago would be on a remote airfield where the fans would be unable to see them.

Said Paul: "We had been told that Chicago had given its blessing to any size crowd greeting us at the main airfield. Figures like 50,000 people being there had been mentioned. Then, a few hours ago, we were calmly informed by some Chicago city official that they hadn't enough police to guarantee protection, so he had ordered the plans altered, and we have to go in by the back door.

"It was a similar case when we arrived in Milwaukee. The crowd was only about 500, we were told, and most of them had been there many hours, waiting to see us arrive. But the police wouldn't let us even drive over to them after making us land a mile away."

Paul went on to declare emphatically: "We are going to use every means at our disposal from now on, television, radio and newspapers, to let everybody know that it isn't our fault the fans aren't being allowed to see us.

"It's a great big drag and we are hating it because we feel it's unnecessary. All this protection is strangling our tour, but we are helpless to prevent it."

All four Beatles had inoculations before last night's show in Milwaukee for sore throat trouble.

John Lennon is worst hit, and missed an earlier press conference on a doctor's advice to rest as much as possible. Yet their performance was well up to top standard.

Ringo on the run at 2am

TUESDAY, SEPTEMBER 8 – They nearly got Ringo at 2am yesterday as The Beatles swept into Canada to the greatest welcome of their tour.

Ten thousand fans crammed the airport. Thousands more lined the streets. And Canadian cops and Mounties whisked The Beatles into town.

At their hotel, 3,000 fans packed the pavement. Hundreds more jammed behind barricades in the lobby.

As The Beatles went in with Ringo at the back, the fans exploded through the police.

Paul scraped through with pieces ripped off his shirt. But three girls clutched Ringo and police pulled them off.

Tonsil pledge from Starr

MONDAY, SEPTEMBER 14 – Ringo Starr promised yesterday that he would bring his tonsils back to Britain.

Rumours had been spreading that he was down with tonsillitis again – and that he would be having them out in America.

But in Boston, where The Beatles appeared before 15,000 yesterday, Ringo explained he would probably wait until after Christmas.

He said: "They feel fine now. Lovely." And John Lennon cracked: "A fan wrote to ask if she could have them after the operation."

Souveniring has reached near-criminal proportions on this wild 15,000-mile swing through the States. The fans, and even the police guarding The Beatles, think anything the boys own is public property.

The Beatles are doing a show in Pittsburgh. Then it's on to Cleveland, New Orleans, Kansas City, Dallas, with a last show in New York.

Giant toys galore

WEDNESDAY, SEPTEMBER 16 – Pictured (above right) is Ringo Starr larking about with two of the many giant toy animals which fans have sent him during The Beatles' American tour.

With them come notes asking Ringo to take the toys wherever he goes.

"If I did that," says Ringo, "I'd need three planes."

RINGO SHARE: Ringo finds a cuddly friend to smoke with – one of many soft toys he received from adoring fans

YOU SAY GOODBYE, AND I SAY HELLO: Waving goodbye at Kennedy Airport before (right) arriving back in London

THE LOST TOUR DIARY

Fallen tree almost causes disaster

The Beatles came within inches of disaster in Florida.

Their limousine, escorted by police motorcyclists at 60mph through hurricane-hit Jacksonville to the airport after their show at the Alligator Bowl, swept round a bend to find a giant tree across the road. The police sergeant ahead swerved his motorcycle violently in a 20-yard skid to miss the obstacle.

The Beatles' car, and mine immediately behind it, came to a halt with tyres screaming as both drivers jammed on their brakes.

The tree had obviously been one of hundreds uprooted by Hurricane Dora the previous day. It had somehow held up until shortly before our car cavalcade came down the road, before crashing to the ground without warning.

Winds remained high following Hurricane Dora and made The Beatles' task on stage immensely difficult. Ringo Starr told me later: "Now and again I thought I was going to be blown right off the stage. It was the worst experience I've had."

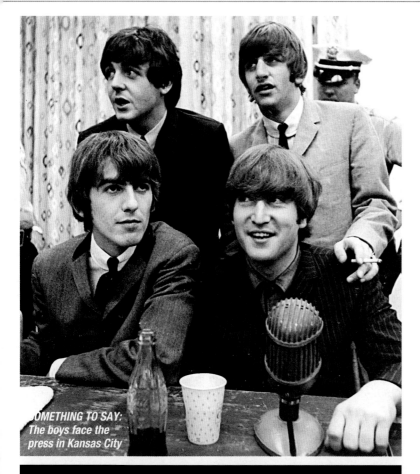

OMETHING TO SAY:
The boys face the
press in Kansas City

Beatles fans take the field

FRIDAY, SEPTEMBER 18 – Police raced madly about a football field in New Orleans on Wednesday, bringing down delirious Beatle fans with flying tackles.

About 500 girls and boys charged across the grass to reach the stage in the middle of the arena where the group were performing.

There were only about 150 police to control them. And in the middle of the crazy melee, John Lennon broke off singing and boomed into his mic: "Who's winning?"

Peace came when the fans became worn out trying to dodge the police. But the police were worn out, too.

Then, after the show, there was another outburst as The Beatles' car was surrounded. Mounted police had to clear a way.

Welcome home!

TUESDAY, SEPTEMBER 22 – The Beatles are home...their triumphant tour of America ended in a passionate welcome from their British fans last night.

Screaming and singing, 8,000 youngsters swept forward as Paul, Ringo, John and George stepped down from their jet at London Airport.

Desperate police fought to save frenzied girls from hurling themselves off the observation platforms as the smiling pop idols waved from the gangway.

Then, within minutes, the four boys were rushed to their waiting car.

For the fans, who started gathering at the airport nine hours before the arrival time, it had been a hard day's wait.

They swarmed over the airport building, chanting: "We love you, Beatles!" and "Ringo for President!"

The Beatles had survived equally ecstatic scenes as they left New York's Kennedy Airport at the end of their 30-day tour which has earned them well over a million dollars.

A reporter asked Ringo what would be the first thing he would do on arriving in London. He replied: "Get off the plane."

George rumours

Rumours of George Harrison's engagement to actress Patti Boyd hit The Beatles' tour before we left Cleveland.

George flatly denied widespread yarns that he's going to announce his engagement to Patti on his return to England next Monday.

This story probably began because he has been spending hundreds of dollars on telephone calls to London every week. Reporters over here reckon George has run up a bill of more than £300 so far on phoning England to speak to Patti, and they figure that nobody would spend that kind of money unless there was something serious between them.

George won't discuss it. To him, it's nobody's business but his own who he telephones or what he spends.

Dallas bomb scare

The Beatles, still in good humour after the roughest welcome of their North American tour, sent 11,000 fans into ear-splitting ecstasy at a Dallas, Texas, concert.

About two hours before the performance, an anonymous telephone bomb threat was received by police, but a check of the auditorium produced nothing.

A LOVE AFFAIR THAT'S LASTED FOR HALF A CENTURY

A relationship based on mutual affection

The Beatles' American love affair would prove to be long-lasting.

It was rekindled with further tours in 1965 and 1966 and, in keeping with the 1964 visits, they were to prove landmark moments in the band's history.

Beatlemania was still in full swing when the boys touched down in New York in August 1965, receiving the now traditional raucous welcome from thousands of devoted fans, who were kept well away from the plane as it landed at John F Kennedy Airport.

The tour opened with an historic performance at Shea Stadium, the first music concert of any kind to take place in a major stadium. It broke records for attendance (over 55,000) and revenue generation (over $300,000).

Film of the event shows many in the crowd to be totally overcome with emotion, with hysterical screaming all but drowning out the sound of The Beatles' performance.

They would go on to play another 15 concerts before the end of the month, and were watched by 325,000 people along the way.

For John, Paul, George and Ringo, a highlight of the trip was a visit to Elvis Presley at his home in Beverly Hills.

The 1966 tour would be more fraught and also marked the end of an era.

There was huge controversy in advance when John Lennon commented that The Beatles were more popular than Jesus Christ, provoking a furious reaction in the bible-belt southern states of America.

Some radio stations refused to play The Beatles' music, while the Ku Klux Klan led a campaign to have concerts cancelled.

Two shows in Memphis on August 19 were initially called off by the city council but they eventually went ahead. A firecracker was thrown on the stage during one of the performances, momentarily alarming the boys who thought the sound they heard was gunfire.

While there were no major incidents during their stay – a Lennon apology helped calm matters – it was a hugely unsettling period and was certainly a contributing factor in The Beatles' decision to retreat to the studio after this tour.

The August 29 show at San Francisco's

AT HOME: The boys pose for photos in New York – a city John Lennon set up home in

BACK AGAIN: The Beatles set off on their fourth visit to America in 1966 while (below) Paul plays the tourist in Miami

Candlestick Park would prove to be their final concert performance.

Although they would never return together to the States, all four Beatles would retain lasting affection for the US.

Paul McCartney and Ringo Starr both married Americans, with Paul rarely apart from Linda Eastman from 1969 until her death from cancer in 1998. His third wife, Nancy Shevell, is a New Yorker. Ringo has been married to actress Barbara Bach since 1981.

John Lennon famously set up home in New York with Yoko Ono from 1971, overcoming attempts to deport him by the Nixon administration who took issue with his opposition to the Vietnam war.

Lennon adored the place, revelling in the energy and colour but appreciating the freedom to go about his business largely undisturbed. Tragically this would all end on the evening of December 8 1980, when he was shot and killed outside his Dakota Building home by Mark Chapman.

George Harrison also spent long periods in America and, sadly, he also died there, succumbing to lung cancer in Los Angeles in November 2001.

Both past their 70th birthdays, Paul and Ringo continue to perform sold-out shows in the US on a regular basis, notably at the recent Grammy celebration.

The timeless quality of The Beatles' music ensures they retain huge popularity with new generations who can't help but be entranced by their magnificent back catalogue.

Their American legacy is neatly summed up by a banner displayed at Shea Stadium during that final 1966 tour: 'Yesterday, Today and Always'.